The Whale's Alibi

60 haiku

Alan Summers

cover photograph

Greenland right whale (Balaena mysticetus)
The mystic whale

Photograph:
The jawbones of a Greenland Right Whale, c.1912
These jaw bones, each measuring approximately 4.10m (13 ft), were part of a specimen from Lochend, Shetland, donated in 1911 by a Mr Haldane.
ID: 3707

Are right whales smart?
Whale and dolphin brains contain specialized brain cells called spindle neurons. These are associated with advanced abilities such as recognising, remembering, reasoning, communicating, perceiving, adapting to change, problem-solving and understanding. So it seems they are deep thinkers!
whales dot org

The Whale's Alibi

Landmarks

creeping sepia
a hint of forbidden sea
in the forest

---

creeping sepia:
The transition into Autumn (Fall) as Summer fades, and growing mixture of an accelerated climate change during the current Anthropocene Epoch. This is also nostalgia when the Seasons were easily defined and experienced.

heat lightning
the rain on the grass
reflects each strike

Atlas foothills…
bees jostle pickers
for saffron

Tides & Sails

intertidal zone–
the waves within lovers
during moonfall

"This is a beautiful haiku, so intricately interconnected. To me, the ambiguity emerges in not knowing exactly where the motion we feel begins and ends. It seems to move, Möbius-like, from the tides outsides us to the inner tides and back again, all under the pull of the moon. I love the duality of "intertidal zone," which again could point to an external place or something entirely internal to the lover in each of us." —**Autumn Noelle Hall**

white sails...
a wind has also shaped
the tree

Depths
&
Seabeds

an owl's moon
watering the black
between stars

"A beautiful, highly suggestive poem. The 'owl's moon' in the opening line seems to refer to the well-known children's picture book by Jane Yolen (Philomel Books, 1987), suggesting an almost fairy-tale setting for the poem itself. In my opinion, the key to reading this haiku lies in the verb 'watering' placed at the beginning of line 2, which overflows in the two closing lines, both physically and ideally filling the space between one star and the other in the night sky.

The 'black between stars' evokes a sense of unfathomable depth (yū 幽), opposed to the faint moonlight that's inexorably destined to fade at dawn.

Note the alliteration of the large and soft 'o' sound in the first line and the 'e' vowel in 'between', suggesting an idea of loosening and flow."

Luca's Lily Pad weekly column – My Haiku Pond (July 2019)
Luca Cenisi, President Emeritus *dell'Associazione Italiana Haiku* (2012-2016)

escape velocity
the moon pulls oceans
behind Apollo 11

a riverbed
of unfulfilled wishes
starry starry night

Weird Numbers

recurringdream#16.333iso/overbreakfast

This is a multiple-pun, a type of *paronomasia*, forgive me, from ISO in photography to other numbers & puns such as *.333 recurring* in long division (arithmetic) repeating decimals as a way to represent something rational. This is also, partly, a riff from John Lennon's *No. 9 Dream* where *"Ah! böwakawa poussé, poussé"* came to him in a dream, and may have no specific meaning.

Where some of us dream of flying, this is part of a MIT Course Number: *16.333* for a lecture on V/STOL stability, dynamics; plus control during transition from hover to forward flight; parameter sensitivity etc...

In addition, there is an Ordnance Survey streetmap by Google with a blue space with the pin in its middle. Also there is the latitude of *Sainte-Rose* which is *16.333 degrees North*; or it alludes to Fukushima via Post-irradiation Analyses of Nuclear Fuels where nuclear power plants go to obtain isotopic compositions and burnups.

almost 10 quintillion insects on Earth at all times maintain radio silence

Isekai dreams
I tread as lightly as rain
in District 9

"Line two is so achingly beautiful! Line one names a Japanese genre that puts ordinary people in otherworldly places, so we know this dream has unsettled the dreamer. The allusion to a movie where interstellar aliens are quarantined on Earth rounds out this expression of modern day alienation. As quickly as the world can change, we can all be thrown into the role of itinerant with little warning."
— Craig Kittner

Author's Note:
Some of us have had lucid dreams. I've experienced them both, while 'asleep,' and also while actually awake, when walking down a main street in the afternoon, as a parallel world unfolded and kept pace alongside me. I was researching for a novel using lucid dreaming as a theme, and device, though I decided to abandon it for various practical reasons.

Isekai (Japanese: 異世界, transl. "different world"): a sub-genre of Japanese fantasy novels, manga, animé, and video games, revolving around a normal person from Earth being transported to, and reborn or trapped, into a parallel universe.

District 9 is an iconic movie that uses science fiction *tropes* to explain our own 'internal' phobias about 'accidental travellers.'

Fox Signals

snowflakes
but for the red
of this fox

a dog fox slips
into snowflakes…
blackbird-braille

after Kate Bush

wind-loaded snow
the shapes foxed
by morning

foxhole
how the snow forgives
and takes away

thunder snow
the wind-shifting scent
of fox

homeward road…
the fox's marks linger
around a snowbank

Fog, Mist, & Dew

mist and dog
the weather forecast
for today

Toshugu shrine pines
I try to stay as still–
mist and dew

Toshugu shrine pines:
Matsuo Bashō and Kawai Sora visited the shrine on the First Day of the Fourth Month (the first day of Summer). Mist and dew are kigo for Spring and Autumn, which I use as a metaphor for our beginnings and endings, and *our lives in-between.* An allusion is also made to Bash'ōs famous saying about learning from the pine trees. —**Alan Summers**

mist haze–
a crow cleans its beak
on a rooftop aerial

distant foghorn
the shark suggests
a good dentist

cumulo, cumulo
the rook and chimney
gleam with dew

Rêves de Neige

snowball vocabulary
we first start by beginning
and ending as snow

christmas globe
the snowdrift teases
at both sides

porch side mountains
the wind-pushed snow
all around us

jackdaws in snow
thumbing through
all our dreams

Commentary by Luca Cenisi:

A haiku set in winter time (*fuyu* 冬), inspired by various Japanese woodblock printings such as *Crow on Snowy Branch* by Watanabe Seitei, and *Two crows in snow* by Ito Sozan, and *Crows in Snow* by Takahashi Biho.

The dark plumage of the jackdaw (*nishikokumarugarasu* 西黒丸烏) stands in stark contrast to the whiteness of the snow (*yuki* 雪), making it clearly visible even at a distance. As underlined by the poet himself, *'jackdaws in a dream can mean positive things including finding love, and that's been a driving force in my life'*; a positive symbol that can be shared by each reader, inscribed within classic aesthetic coordinates.

Note the semi-vowel 'w' in line 1, which gives a sense of openness and softness to the opening line, and the reiteration of the sound 'th' in the following line, which effectively renders the sense of revelation underlying this poem.

a flink of cows
the blue before a night
of falling snow

a light snow
drifting into the eaves. . .
earl grey with lemon

there are times
when we are graced
snowlight

Twelve cows are a flink.

Radar

changing skylines . . .
a tree bumblebee climbs
the heuchera flower

wild wood
the robins testing
their song

野生森
駒鳥は試す
彼らの歌を

Or

野生森 駒鳥は試す 彼らの歌を

Translated by Hasegawa Kai
Founder of Japanese haiku circle and journal *Koshi.*

Moonfall

last cup of tea
a time of moonfall
with the mountain

moonfall–
the waves
within us

duskfall…
the moon bumps
into a paperboat

"It's difficult sometimes to summarize a whole story into the shortest possible amount of words, but when someone does it, it becomes a masterpiece. This haiku is one of those masterpieces . . ."
—**Hifsa Ashraf** (Pakistan)

"Another feeling I get from this haiku is the beauty of the "o" sounds in "moon," "into," and "paperboat." These long syllables slow down the poem and create the scene of dusk potently. It's difficult to write an original haiku about the moon after 100s of years of tradition of doing so. Mr. Summers has done it through his unique juxtaposition, word choice, and imagery."
—**Nicholas Klacsanzky** (Ukraine/USA)

Recognised as a "*Highly Rated Poem"* in **The Readers 'Choice Awards** 2019
The Heron's Nest (online Quarterly, and print Annual)

moonshot
Planet B
swerves

Commentary by Robert Kingston:

"I find myself. . .believing sometimes he is writing in a unique form of binary language. Albeit in a light and succinct manner."

moonshot

"The first line clearly speaks of man's attempt at another (some doubt we did it before) moon landing. So desperate are we, that enemies on earth congregate to seek out our future home together."

Planet B

"The pivot, deliberately made cryptic in order to cause thought. I found myself turning to Google to go beyond "b" believing I found an intention to expand in a 70's fiction film titled 'planet B'."

swerves

"Line three for me sums up the sceptics. The ones to whom many people turn, in order to detract from providing their energy to further boost our efforts in protecting this ever so diverse planet. For me Alan's is an expansive poem, joyful to explore, though filled with sadness and a desperate call for food for thought."

Alan says: *Planet B* is also a 2024 dystopian science fiction thriller film, directed & written by Aude Léa Rapin: It stars Adèle Exarchopoulos as an activist who awakens on a mysterious planet.

Starboard

vesper flights
the ever-falling blue
of swifts

on the trail
of a heron
riverbend

Glimpses

riverlight
the sewing pins
of rainfall

riverlight commentaries

Commenting on a master's haiku is always a gamble, but fundamentally…*fortuna adiuvat audaces*. At first, I wondered what the light of the river was: The brightness of the river's surface or the lights on its shore … then I realized that it didn't really matter and that I didn't have to rationalize too much.

The image that reaches me is immediate: dark, a light that reflects on the river and on falling raindrops. The raindrops, if illuminated by an intense light in the dark, can highlight and hypnotically catalyze the eye. Enlightenment that reveals what would otherwise escape us. And here, they are clearly evident: these thin needles that sew the river with the sky, the darkness with darkness, in a single landscape.

This haiku, masterfully expressed in a few words, has enchanted someone like me who loves brevity very much. I also enjoy its harmonious fluidity, which cleverly breaks into a stark tone only in the second line. It harmonizes well with an Italian who is accustomed to the harmonious sounds of their own language. —**Margherita Petriccione** (Italy)

Riverlight, with its great mystery, is used as the starting note of this beautiful orchestral haiku, where the subtlety of life lies in the light that makes no difference to the flowing water but to the falling rain. The analogy of sewing pins with rainfall makes this haiku poignant and profound. The synthesis of sight, touch, and feel in this haiku makes it more profound and mystical in nature, where the light turns rain into painful experiences or trials of life that eventually lead to eternal peace.
—**Hifsa Ashraf** (Pakistan)

One of the great qualities of Alan's work is that it is always unique and often imaginative/abstract. However, this imagination is grounded in the perception of reality." *riverlight"* is a good example of this. The invented word in the first line and the image of rainfall being like sewing pins can be easily understood. In some instances, rain does appear to be sharp and could be mistaken for sewing pins. Though sewing pins can be seen as something sharp, they can also be perceived as something that mends the broken. This may be why "riverlight" is used: the rain has merged the river and sunlight/moonlight.

Also, Alan might be saying that riverlight is akin to the magic of rain appearing as sewing pins. In terms of sound, the "i" jumps out in almost every word in this haiku. They are in the shape of sharp rain and even have a sonic comparison to them. I also like the format, with the second line setting up a surprise in the third line.

Overall, I believe this poem is unique, fascinating, and economically written.
—**Nicholas Klacsanzky** (Ukraine/USA)

Mȳthos

night of small colour
a part of the underworld
becomes one heron

This haiku is classified as mythopoetic reality. The mythopoesis [is] evident in the semantic twist of "small colour" of night, a part of which "becomes one heron." What lies between realism and imagination, between living and dreaming, [as] a particular form of sanctuary; a space of poiesis. It seems most fragile and nuanced, insignificant and ephemeral—yet it calls or we call, in seeking deeper, more enriching, increasingly multiple, multifarious dimensions of knowing in psyche.

Wallace Stevens refers to this poetical process as "enlargement".

—Richard Gilbert, Japan
Poetry as Consciousness - Haiku Forests, Space of Mind, and an Ethics of Freedom
(Keibunsha, Japan 2018)

"Invoking a "third" reality or poetic space occurs frequently in poetry—though as mythopoesis, is not overtly given in the text; under purview is the phenomenology of reader reception. Each of these examples points to a "third" realm of being in consciousness—at some distance."
Relating to *small colour*...in Alan Summers' the whispered and distant "third" space of "*just your.*"

—Richard Gilbert, Japan
Haiku Sanctuary, Between Living and Dreaming
(Kumamoto Studies in English Language and Literature 61, 2019, Japan)

The Rickety Man

autumn deepens
alongside the rickety man…
scudding clouds

This *ku* comes from the fact that he recently got awful sciatica, which resulted from a damage or injury to his sciatic nerve, causing very intense pain in the back and a consequent, reduced mobility.

The clouds (*kumo* 雲) in line 3 therefore become a sort of guide during his rehab process, thanks to their regular and straight movement that allowed him to always have a reference during his daily walks.

The autumn season (*aki* 秋), on the other hand, clearly refers to the fact that the poet feels aged and overwhelmed by various kind of aches; it 'deepens' (*susumu* 進む) just like the protagonist's pain, picturing a situation that is both personal and universal. —**Luca Cenisi**

Crocodile
Tick Tock

a hot cocoa swirls
by the ticking crocodile
overdue book fines

Commentary by Craig Kittner:

Alan Summers supersaturates his haiku with time:
The cocoa is hot now, but will cool. It's swirling now, but will stop. Each tick of the crocodile's swallowed clock is a *second* gone.

The book is overdue, and each day adds to the fine. And what is Peter's story, but a refusal to accept time's inevitability and all the forces aligned against that refusal?

Alan, if you are truly in *Neverland*, please send better directions. I can never figure out which star is the second from the right!

erratic rainfall
the deliveryman buys
an alligator pear

Allegedly the avocado has been called many names and has a skin similar to a swamp beast.

The Rill's Trick

the rill's trick
a greenfinch moves
its green around

Contest Judges, Lorin Ford / Lee Gurga, Haiku Society of America:

The sound of this haiku is a delight.

The rill (in a village Green or a field, we imagine, of Spring-green grass) reflects its surroundings as it trickles along.

The little green bird, busy catching small insects along the rill to take back to its nest, is detectable only by its movements.

The repeated assonance of the small *i* sound and the two instances of "green" add to the rhythm and make this haiku sing like a birdsong. One could whistle it!

This is a fresh haiku which illustrates Basho's "*karumi/ lightness*" aesthetic very well indeed. A puzzle is presented to the reader: what is the "*rill's trick?*"

Perhaps the rill reflects the bird and this tricks it into perceiving there's another greenfinch, a competitor: the greenfinch may very well be trying to chase its own reflection away!

Skónis

an attic window sill
a wasp curls
into its own dust

Nicholas Klacsanzky (Ukraine/USA):
To me, the act of the wasp curling into its own dust is representative of an attic itself: self-contained, enclosed, and a place of possible loneliness. The wasp being at the windowsill adds more to the pathos of this haiku, as it indicates that the wasp wished to leave the stuffy attic for its free life outside.

Hifsa Ashraf (Pakistan):
The connection between 'attic' and 'dust' shows the stages of maturity that we gain phase by phase and eventually gain the maturity level where the outcomes of those experiences become our strength and protect us from an unseen future.

'Dust 'may also reflect the annihilation where a person bends down due to either ageing or the brunt of the past that they bury under the dust of time or death.

The articles 'an' and 'a' project the individual experiences of a person that are more subtle but profound. The letter 'w', I feel, gives a sense of the ups and downs in life that reshape our intellect and bring ultimate maturity until death.

shift of waves
pilot whales navigate
a Sahara dust storm

mars landing–
a tendril of red dust
shifts from a footfall

a little blue dust
on the mantelpiece
all that’s left

the shoemaker
adds his own dust
moon dreams

stardust . . .
the humans quietly
reassemble

we slip under
into the faery realms
yew cemetery

Port

wild peppermint
a dock leaf shadow
clings to the bee

when the great whale
is revealed cell by cell...
low tide

Alan Summers 'haiku at once creates a scene that we usually see in real life, scenes we know are haunting but can't look away.

The great whale took all my attention in the initial reads, an image of a giant creature beached on the shore dominates. How long was it dead? Is it a full carcass or just bones? The other two lines are temporarily overshadowed by the ghastliness of it all.

But then I realized this haiku speaks a lot more about the momentum of the sea than it does about the beached giant. The globe spanning ocean retreats from the shore so slowly that it reveals the great whale cell by cell.

This pitting of the enormous with the slow is so striking. The idea of whale carcass on the shore made all the more stirring.

—**Sankara Jayanth**, editor, Haiku Seed Journal

thunder
I slide a kigo
into the gun

Marion Clarke unveils the cinematic:

A fine haiku from Alan Summers that comes with a soundtrack! We are presented with the rumble of thunder in the first line, that also conjures up an image of a threatening sky. Intriguingly, in line two we learn that the speaker is sliding a kigo — but what does this mean? Then we discover that it is being slid into a gun and imagine that action and hear the click of a gun being loaded. Thunder is a Summer kigo, so we know the air is very close before a cloudburst, and might imagine cool metal against a hot palm. And, who knows, perhaps a hint of gunpowder hangs in the air.

On a second reading, I wondered if the gun has been loaded with a kigo of more favorable weather, such as "blue skies" or a "burning sun" that will blast away those threatening skies.

Peggy Bilbro reacts as a poet and a warrior:

Odd that Alan used the word slide because that is what my mind wants to do every time I read this poem. It wants to slide away from the gun, the bullet, and the sounds of war that all underlie the words. I try to concentrate on the distant thunder of an approaching storm, the observation of seasons and the idea of a poem as a weapon against the injustices of life, but am constantly pulled back to the chilling vision of impending war.

It seems that Alan has caught the perfect balance that forces the reader to exist between the implicit and the explicit, wishes and facts, creation and destruction, poet and warrior. This is a poem that will stay with me for a very long time.

Patchwork Extinction

rain-soaked wind
the weather-worn notice
peels back more

patchwork elephant
just a throw cushion away
from extinction

Lūminōsus

leaves of a book...
travelling the blue atlas
on ember clouds

old tales
moon-bright leaves
jostle the breeze

drifting rain
my hundred autumn rooms
to be alone

each of us born
with a number of breaths–
swallow flight

deep end of winter
a swan's luminosity
enters the river

Epilégō

“Haiku is the universe wrapped up small.”
—Alan Summers (November 2023)

“There are no useless words or phrases. A perfect haiku.”
Isamu Hashimoto (Japan, 2014)
Selector for The Mainichi's popular Haiku in English column

"Widely known haiku poet...as dry as vintage champagne”
Yomiuri Shimbun (14 million readers in Japan)
(On my September birthday in 2002, as I was in Tokyo.)

“Astonishingly moving haiku”
Yomiuri Shimbun Language Lab (Japan 2005)

“One can taste Alan Summers’ poetry on the tongue.
It has a special, memorable taste.”
—Kati Mohr, Germany

Alan Summers
founder, Call of the Page
www.callofthepage.org

Jushō-reki
受賞歴

an attic window sill
Haiku of Merit awarded by Professor Hoshino Tsunehiko:
Ginko & Kukai event (1997)

Also:
Yomiuri Shimbun, Japan, especially for my birthday in September, 2002
while I was in Tokyo.

heat lightning
1st Prize, The Liverpool Virtual Book Fair Twitter Haiku Contest 2014
(part of the city's International Festival of Business)

deep end of winter
1st Prize, (English Section)
Societatea Română de Haiku Contest (2019)

the rill's trick
3rd Place, 2018 Henderson Haiku Contest (Haiku Society of America)

wild wood
Honourable Mention
2nd Oku-no-hosomichi Soka Matsubara International Haiku Competition
(Japan 2022) selected by Hasegawa Kai

drifting rain
Awarded Best of Mainichi 2012 (Isamu Hashimoto, Japan)

wild peppermint
Commended, The Basho Museum Memorial Anthology, Ueno, Japan 2001
Selected by Tadashi Kondo

Thank you for helping to find the book cover image, which is perfect!

Karen Hoy

Thank you for the people who supported me off and on over the decades:

Ikkoku Santo
Hoshino Tsunehiko
Isamu Hashimoto
Susumu Takiguchi
Janice Bostok
Merrill Ann Gonzales
Fay Aoyagi
Autumn Noelle Hall

Thanks for quotes, commentaries, and support

Kati Mohr
Hifsa Ashraf
Sankara Jayanth
Luca Cenisi
Richard Gilbert
Lee Gurga
Scott Metz
Craig Kittner
Hasegawa Kai
Jacob Salzer
Nicholas Klacsanzky
Robert Kingston
Margherita Petriccione
Marion Clarke
Peggy Bilbro
Michael Smeer

Acknowledgements

Azami journal founder and editor Ikkoku Santo (Japan); Five Fleas Itchy Poetry, fleakeeper, Robin/Roberta Beach Jacobson; Liverpool Virtual Book Fair & the International Festival of Business; kjmunro, A Sense of Place (Haiku Foundation); Craig Kittner of Poet's Choice, Ambiguity (Haiku Foundation); Faces and Place ed. Don Baird (The Little Buddha Press 2015); a procession of ripples, an anthology of selected haiku ed. laryalee fraser (2006); Meet… Alan Summers (interview by Gilles Fabre) for Seashores journal; The Living Haiku Anthology editors; Leaf-fall ed. Akira Yagami; Luca's Lily Pad: a weekly column by Luca Cenisi (Founder/former President, Italian Haiku Association, and the European Haiku Society); The Comfort of Crows (Hifsa Ashraf and Alan Summers) published by Chrissi Villa of Velvet Dusk Publishing; "Rocket Dreams" Commission for U.K. National Poetry Day (October 200)7 with Space Historian Piers Bizony and NASA images, part of World Space Week; Bloo Outlier Journal; fox dreams ed. Aubrie Cox; the way of the itinerant ed Craig Kittner; Red ed Thomas Haynes; Shrikaanth Krishnamurthy and ephemerae; Beginning: British Haiku Society Members 'Anthology 2016 editor Shrikaanth Krishnamurthy; Temps Libre Coups de coeur, Serge Tomé; Caduceus poetry feature editor Dawn Gorman; best haiga ed. Lavana Kray; "Photographs and Words" with Stewart Wall, Royal Photographic Society; Our Garden: The Haiku Foundation Volunteers Anthology 2022 ed. Jim Kacian & Julie Bloss Kelsey; World Haiku Series (Japan) curated by Hideori Hiruta; Commissioned video presentation SHAHAI The art of three: photography; haiku; typography; Hermitage ed. Ion Codrescu (Romania); World Haiku Review Japan Article – Vending machines and cicadas; Travelogue on World Haiku Festival 2002 Part 1 (Akita International Haiku Network, Japan); We Are All Japan ed. Robert D. Wilson & Saša Važić (Karakia Press); The In-Between Season (With Words Pamphlet); Haiku Sansaar; First Australian Online Anthology; Cornell University, Mann Library, U.S.A. "Daily Haiku" poet curated by Tom Clausen; Watermark: A Poet's Notebook - Crows ed. Sharon Brogan; Grandmother's Pearls: An Anthology of Dream Poems ed. Alexis Rotella (Jade Mountain Press, 2021); Heliosparrow, Richard Gilbert; Asahi Shimbun (Japan); Harusame ed. Luca Cenisi; entering the earth (EarthRise Rolling Haiku Collaboration 2021); THF Per Diem (2021) curated by Iliyana Stoyanova; Blithe Spirit (journal of British Haiku Society); Presence journal; The Heron's Nest; tinywords; The Wise Owl Haiku Renditions Zoom companion collection ed. Neena Singh & Alan Summers; Haiku Commentary series ed. Nicholas Klacsanzky, Hifsa Ashraf & Jacob Salzer; Naviar Records, Marco Sebastiano Alessi; Opposites Attract – day/night ed. kjmunro; Desert Rain Haiku Nook: An Anthology (2022); Modern Haiku journal (USA) ed. Paul Miller; Haiku 2015 (Modern Haiku Press, 2015); Poetry as Consciousness - Haiku Forests, Space of Mind, and an Ethics of Freedom, Richard Gilbert pub. Keibunsha (Japan); Haiku Sanctuary, Between Living and Dreaming by Professor Richard Gilbert, Kumamoto Studies in English Language and Literature (Kumamoto University 2019, Japan); Brass Bell Showcase: Alan Summers (2015) ed. Zee Zahava; Yanty's Butterfly Haiku Nook: An Anthology (2016) ed. Jacob Salzer & Nook Editorial Staff; Under the Bashō, Don Baird, Editor-in-Chief; borrowed books ed. Craig Kittner; Stardust Haiku ed. Valentina Ranaldi-Adams; frogpond (journal of Haiku Society of America); Haiku Foundation's New to Haiku: Advice for Beginners – Alan Summers; Woodpecker Special Extra Shuttle Issue (Netherlands 1997); Swot, arts & literature magazine, Bath Spa University (2007); First Australian Online Haiku Anthology (1999); Haiku International 2000 Anthology (Japan 2000); The Omnibus Anthology, Haiku and Senryu, Hub Editions ed. Fred Schofield (2001); The New Haiku (Snapshot Press, 2002); Raku Teapot: Haiku Book and CD (Raku Teapot Press in association with White Owl Publishing Book, 2003); First Australian Haiku Anthology (Paper Wasp 2003); Dylan Tweney "Practical Haiku: How Reading and Writing an Ancient Form of Poetry Can Change Your Life."; Haiku Scout Report (Andrew Dugas); The Moon is Broken: Juxtaposition in haiku (Fellowship of Australian Writers, Queensland); WASHOKU - Japanese Food Culture and Cuisine ed. Dr Gabi Greve (Japan); Haiku Seed Journal (2022) ed. Sankara Jayanth; Trash Panda, Lisa Anne Johnson; Haiku 2021 ed. Scott Metz & Lee Gurga (Modern Haiku Press, 2021); Southern California Haiku Study Group (2021); THF re:Virals 283 (2021); Judges 'Favorites, Selected Haiku 6th annual Golden Haiku Competition (The Golden Triangle Business Improvement District, Washington DC, USA, 2019); throw pillow ed. Craig Kittner; cattails Premier Edition Tribute Page to John E. Carley, Principal editor an'ya, USA (January 2014); Wild Plum ed. Gabriel Sawicki; Vast Sky, An Anthology of Contemporary World Haiku (Tancho Press 2015) ed. Bruce Ross; Koko Kato; Dietmar Tauchner & Patricia Prime; The Haiku Foundation Per Diem's melancholy ed. Sandi Pray; Pulse—voices from the heart of medicine (inaugural haiku issue ed. Neal Whitman, October 2013); Journal of Romanian-Japanese cultural interferences HAIKU (Bucharest, Romania). Societatea Română de Haiku, Vasile Moldovan; The Basho Museum Memorial Anthology (Japan)

ISBN: 978-93-6354-565-6

First Edition: 2024
Rs. 200/-

Cyberwit.net
HIG 45 Kaushambi Kunj, Kalindipuram
Allahabad - 211011 (U.P.) India
http://www.cyberwit.net
E-mail: info@cyberwit.net

Printed at VCORRE PRESS.

www.ingramcontent.com/pod-product-compliance
Lightning Source LLC
Chambersburg PA
CBHW050024170726
48282CB00025B/541
* 9 7 8 9 3 6 3 5 4 5 6 5 6 *